More than Me

Written by Tranae S. Dunn

WestBow Press books may be ordered through booksellers or by contacting:

WestBow Press
A Division of Thomas Nelson & Zondervan
1663 Liberty Drive
Bloomington, IN 47403
www.westbowpress.com
844-714-3454

ISBN: 978-1-6642-6144-0 (sc)
ISBN: 978-1-6642-6146-4 (hc)
ISBN: 978-1-6642-6145-7 (e)

Library of Congress Control Number: 2022905238

Print information available on the last page.

WestBow Press rev. date: 05/05/2022

WESTBOW
PRESS®
A DIVISION OF THOMAS NELSON
& ZONDERVAN

To Our Daughters,

Praying God will use us to inspire you as much as you inspire us.

Love,
Daddy & Mommy

"Follow me as I follow Christ.' -1 Corinthians 11:1

My darling dear, I love you so.
And there is something you should know.
My love for you goes so deep
But someone loves you more than me.

You are delightful and unique.
My heart is filled with glee!
Overflowing with love,
So much you can see.

2

But JESUS, He loves you more than me.

I love you more than shopping at home decor stores,
With candles, throw pillows and knick-knacks galore.

I love you more than relaxing
With coffee or hot tea.
Even so, JESUS
Loves you more than me.

6

I love you more than sleeping in late.
On Saturday mornings you give me a shake.

7

I love you more than
Starry summer
Nights...

8

Or breezy beach
Days when we
Laugh and fly kites.

9

I love the time we share together,
It's so special to me.
Whether we're working on a tough project
Or cheering for our favorite team.

I love you way more than courtside seats
Or preseason games and concession stand eats—
Now that's a whole lot of love!

But even so,
JESUS' love never skips a beat.
His love is unconditional for all
eternity!

I love you more than rainbows that
the spring rain brings.

I love you way more
than shiny gold
things.

15

I love you more than a yummy picnic lunch

Or crisp autumn air and leaves that crunch.

I love you more than the brightes
And most festive Christmas tree

Even so, JESUS
Loves you more than me.

19

We can see in John 3:16,
God's great love for you and me.
He sent His Son from up above,
And there's no greater love
That will ever be!

So my darling dear,
I love you more than I can say.
Because of this love
I ask God when I pray

That as you grow up,
Each day you will see...

Printed in the United States
by Baker & Taylor Publisher Services